AGRIPPINA
"ATROCIOUS AND FEROCIOUS"

By Shirin Yim Bridges | Illustrated by Peter Malone

goosebottombooks

Series editor **Shirin Yim Bridges**
Editor **Amy Novesky**
Copy editor **Jennifer Fry**
Editorial assistant **Ann Edwards**
Book design **Jay Mladjenovic**

Typeset in Trajan, Ringbearer, Volkswagen, and Gill Sans
Illustrations rendered in gouache

Manufactured in Singapore

Library of Congress Control Number: 2011924353

ISBN: 978-0-9834256-1-8

First Edition   10 9 8 7 6 5 4 3 2 1

Goosebottom Books LLC
710 Portofino Lane, Foster City, CA 94404

www.goosebottombooks.com

The Thinking Girl's Treasury of Dastardly Dames

Cleopatra
"Serpent of the Nile"

Agrippina
"Atrocious and Ferocious"

Mary Tudor
"Bloody Mary"

Catherine de' Medici
"The Black Queen"

Marie Antoinette
"Madame Deficit"

Cixi
"The Dragon Empress"

For my mother, the best role model a thinking girl could have. ~ **Shirin Yim Bridges**

"ATROCIOUS AND FEROCIOUS"

It is a clear night in the year 59. A woman sits looking out at the road approaching her imposing seaside villa. Her name is Agrippina. The proud tilt of her chin reflects her status as a great-granddaughter of Augustus, the first Roman emperor. As the sister of the emperor Caligula, and then wife of the emperor Claudius, she has been highly honored, even deified (declared a goddess). But now, to the small group of people watching her villa from the side of the road, she is a monster. They believe that she has poisoned her husbands, sent soldiers to bring back the heads of her enemies, and done other unspeakable things. She knows that they will not help her now, and as dust rises on the road announcing the approach of soldiers, they melt away into the shadows. Agrippina will have to face her murderers alone.

Where she lived

Cologne, Germany, where Agrippina was born.

Rome, center of the Roman Empire.

The Pontine Islands, where Agrippina was exiled.

Misenum, where she was eventually murdered.

When she lived

This timeline shows when the Dastardly Dames were born.

69 BC	15 AD		1516 AD	1519 AD		1755 AD		1835 AD
Cleopatra	Agrippina		Mary Tudor	Catherine de' Medici		Marie Antoinette		Cixi

HER STORY

Agrippina was born on November 6, in the year 15, not in Rome but in Germany, near what is now the city of Cologne. This was where her father, Rome's most popular general, Germanicus, was headquartered. Her mother was a haughty granddaughter of Augustus, the first emperor. As she was also called Agrippina, our Agrippina became known as Agrippina the Younger.

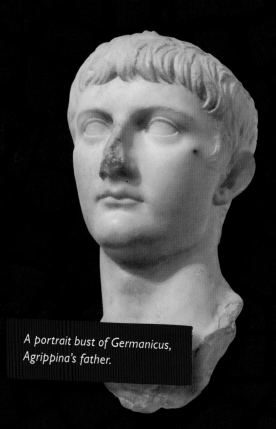

A portrait bust of Germanicus, Agrippina's father.

3

When Agrippina was little more than a year old, her father was recalled to Rome, and honored with a lavish triumph—a grand public procession—after his return. As people swarmed the streets to catch a glimpse of their hero, Agrippina's father drove past in a chariot crowded with his five children: Nero, Drusus, Caligula, Agrippina, and Drusilla. Agrippina tried to keep her balance as the chariot jolted through crowds roaring with excitement, chanting Germanicus' name. The standards and banners of her father's armies snapped in the air. Grain thrown by well-wishers rained down, flecking her hair.

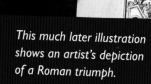

This much later illustration shows an artist's depiction of a Roman triumph.

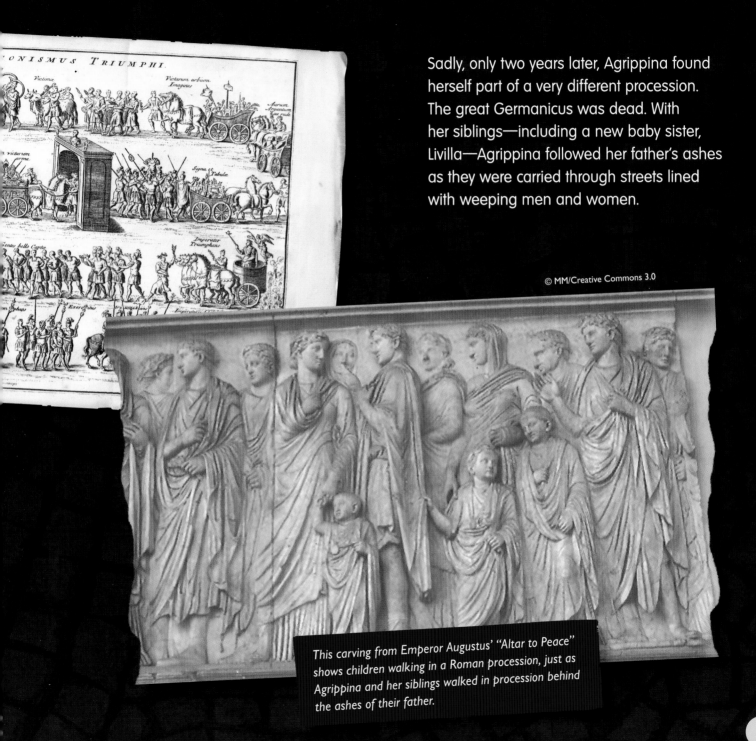

Sadly, only two years later, Agrippina found herself part of a very different procession. The great Germanicus was dead. With her siblings—including a new baby sister, Livilla—Agrippina followed her father's ashes as they were carried through streets lined with weeping men and women.

This carving from Emperor Augustus' "Altar to Peace" shows children walking in a Roman procession, just as Agrippina and her siblings walked in procession behind the ashes of their father.

5

How she lived

Rome's Palatine Hill is where we actually get
the word "palace," because its villas looking
down on the rest of Rome were palatial
indeed. Their floors were covered in intricate
mosaics, their walls painted with murals, and
at the rear, most opened into what are known
as peristyle gardens—gardens surrounded by
a columned and covered walkway where the
family could relax in private.

Nothing could make up for the loss of her father, but at least Agrippina grew up on Rome's prestigious Palatine Hill surrounded by uncles (including the current emperor, Tiberius, a great-uncle), aunts, grandmothers, and even a great-grandmother, which was unusual in Ancient Rome where the average woman only lived to twenty-nine years of age. Then, four years later, the emperor's son, Drusus, died and Agrippina's life took a turn for the worse.

Drusus' death threw into question who would now be heir to the throne. Drusus had left a son, but he was only four years old. Agrippina's eldest brothers, men aged seventeen and sixteen (Romans were usually considered men at the age of fourteen), became obvious candidates for the succession. What followed was a bitter battle between Agrippina's mother, intent on advancing her sons, and Emperor Tiberius, who favored his own grandson.

A portrait bust of Agrippina's mother and namesake—the haughty and headstrong Agrippina the Elder.

The first Roman emperor, Augustus.

The second emperor, Tiberius. He was Augustus' adopted and step-son, but not related to Augustus by blood.

Hiding unnoticed behind the many columns that graced the imperial palaces, Agrippina would have heard the adults cluck their tongues at her mother's incautious behavior. Agrippina the Elder thought that not only their age but their blood link to the first emperor, Augustus, made her sons the more worthy heirs to the imperial throne. Her haughty opinion was offensive to Tiberius, who had been adopted by Augustus. Like his grandson, he was not related to Augustus by blood. Agrippina's proud and headstrong mother was putting herself and her sons in danger.

As the palace gossip predicted, Agrippina's mother and two eldest brothers were dealt with brutally—banished, imprisoned, murdered, or starved. (One of her brothers was said to have eaten the stuffing of his mattress in his terrible desperation.) Agrippina and her shell-shocked sisters were married off to respectable Roman politicians. Despite the disgrace of his family, their remaining brother, Caligula, was summoned to live with Tiberius.

He was called what?!

Caligula's full name was Gaius Julius Caesar Augustus Germanicus, but he was given the nickname Caligula by the soldiers of his father's armies. As a boy, his mother often dressed him up like a little soldier to win the favor of the troops. His outfit included tiny boy-sized hob-nailed boots like the soldiers wore. These earned him the name Caligula, which means "little boots."

At the ripe old age of seventy-seven, Tiberius died and Caligula became the new Roman Emperor. (The senate decided Tiberius' grandson was too young to be heir, so the murderous tussle over the succession had been for nothing.) Agrippina found herself thrust back into the limelight. Her name was included in the annual oaths of loyalty to the emperor, her brother. Caligula even minted coins with his portrait on one side and Agrippina and her sisters on the other. But if Agrippina hoped that the challenges in her life were over, she was sorely disappointed.

© Clio20/Creative Commons 3.0

Caligula fell ill, and by the time he recovered, many thought he had lost his mind. He was suspicious, irrational, and violent—and those who had been closest to him suffered most. Agrippina found herself banished to the same windswept rock where her mother had starved out her final days, accused of plotting to overthrow him. Torn from her young son, friendless and alone, she must have been haunted by her mother's fate as she looked out at the relentless waves. She seemed destined to perish there, just as her mother had. But then, Agrippina's fortunes changed again.

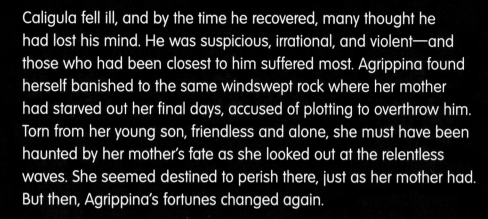

Claudius, discovered cowering behind the curtains, as imagined by Lawrence Alma-Tadema in his painting from 1871.

Caligula was murdered by his own men, the elite Praetorian Guard. It was a great shock at the time, but he would turn out to be only the first of many emperors to suffer this fate. The Guard then pronounced Claudius, the brother of their adored Germanicus, whom they'd found quivering behind a curtain, emperor. The new emperor exonerated his niece—he did more than pardon her, he declared that there was never any guilt in the first place—and Agrippina returned from exile. Might this have been the point when Agrippina's legendary thirst for power began? Having narrowly survived a situation where she had absolutely no control over her fate, she might have been determined never to find herself so vulnerable again. But for the moment, Agrippina wisely kept a low profile. She remarried (her first husband had died of natural causes during her exile), this time to a governor of Rome's Asian territories. Historians think she probably took her son to live abroad with her new husband.

A portrait bust of Agrippina's uncle, Emperor Claudius.

Coins showing the profile of the new emperor.

Agrippina's return to Rome was a dramatic one. In the year 47, the Secular Games were held—a very special event for the Romans, one that was supposed to be celebrated only once every one hundred years. (In reality, the Romans often couldn't wait that long and celebrated them more frequently.) The crowds noticed Agrippina in the stands, aloof and alone (she had been recently widowed again). One highlight of the Games was a parade of the sons of Rome's greatest families—the boys who would one day run the empire—and as the crowds watched, Agrippina's son, Nero, handsome and athletic even at the age of nine, rode by. The people cheered, delighted by how much he looked like his legendary grandfather, Germanicus.

In the imperial box, Emperor Claudius must have noticed how much more popular Nero was than his own son, Britannicus. This great-nephew of his might grow up to become a threat. Claudius had never felt very secure on his throne—he was only there as the result of a military coup. Agrippina now took advantage of this insecurity.

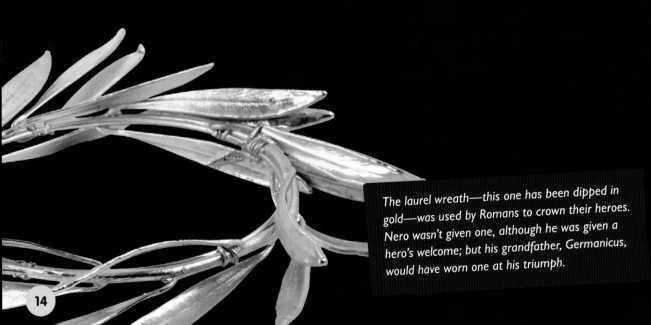

The laurel wreath—this one has been dipped in gold—was used by Romans to crown their heroes. Nero wasn't given one, although he was given a hero's welcome; but his grandfather, Germanicus, would have worn one at his triumph.

Fun and games

The Romans went to great lengths to import exotic animals like lions, hippopotamuses, ostriches, rhinoceroses, crocodiles, elephants, leopards, and bears for their games. With these poor creatures they staged mock hunts, or set two animals against each other in fights to the death, or pitted an animal—or several—against a gladiator. Agrippina's son, Nero, was especially fond of using the big cats as a means of executing Christians. He would literally feed the Christians to the lions as public entertainment.

At the official opening of the Colosseum, in the year 80 (around twenty years after Agrippina's death), 9,000 animals died during a one-hundred-day long festival. And these were only the animals killed on stage. Many more died in transit, before they had a chance to be part of the "fun."

An ancient fresco showing a couple on their wedding night, from a villa, Casa della Farnesina, in Rome. This painting was already thirty-five years old when Agrippina was born.

When Claudius' wife died, palace tongues were soon wagging about how much time Agrippina was spending with her uncle Claudius. What did she say to him in the many close conversations that were observed? Maybe she convinced him that any emperor would be more secure on his throne if he had a viable heir. Nero, then eleven, was almost old enough to play this role, while Britannicus was not. Maybe she hinted that marrying her and adopting Nero would make Nero part of Claudius' own camp. Nero was a valuable ally because, just by being the grandson of Germanicus, he commanded the Praetorian Guard's love and loyalty.

It was illegal in Rome for an uncle to marry his niece, but Claudius and Agrippina had friends argue in the senate that this marriage was important to the welfare of the Roman people. It would give Claudius a respectable wife and a capable mother for his son, Britannicus.

It is interesting that at this point, thirty-four years old and twice widowed, Agrippina could still be held up as an example of respectability. Nobody believed—or had even thought of—the crimes she would later be accused of having committed by this time. In fact, the senate was so convinced that Agrippina would make a good wife, they not only changed the long-standing Roman law, they sent a delegation to ask the emperor to marry Agrippina, as if it had been their own brilliant idea in the first place!

What she wore

1) Statues of Agrippina showed her wearing a diadem in her lifetime, which caused mutterings as diadems were considered signs of divinity, usually allowed to mortals only after death.

2) The long tunic, or chiton, was similar to those worn in Ancient Greece.

3) The stola was only worn by married women and proclaimed their respectability and modesty.

4) The palla was a long cloak that was used to veil the head in public. (The Romans took this seriously. A roman consul named Gallus once divorced his wife for leaving the house with her head unveiled.) Agrippina was reported to have owned an amazing cloak woven with golden threads—another sign of her arrogance as gold was the color of royalty and the people of Rome still liked to think of themselves as a republic.

...bur Agrippina's popularity with the senate was short-lived. Never before had a Roman woman demanded and flaunted so much power! Emperor Augustus' wife, Livia, had been a powerful woman because she had been his trusted advisor, but she had never wielded her power publicly. Agrippina, on the other hand, demanded to be treated like a second emperor.

Within a year of her marriage, Agrippina had been given the title "Augusta"—the highest honor that could be given to an empress, and one that had taken the great Livia a lifetime to earn. Her statues showed her wearing a diadem, a distinction usually reserved for divinities, or given as a mark of respect to mortals after death. Coins showed Agrippina and Claudius side by side, or front and back, equal in majesty. Every morning, when courtiers came to pay homage to the emperor and to ask for favors, they had to pay the same homage to a proud and haughty Agrippina—*atrox ac ferox*, atrocious and ferocius, some called her.

The rumblings of discontent at Agrippina's arrogant behavior reached a peak when the captured British chieftain, Caratacus, was brought to kneel before Claudius. As Claudius looked down from his raised dais, flanked by the Praetorian Guard and surrounded by the standards and emblems of Roman power, Agrippina sat looking down her nose from her own dais beside him.

Claudius and Agrippina are shown as equals, one on each side of this coin.

The more powerful Agrippina became, the more hated she was. Rumors started to fly that she would stop at nothing to get more power. After all, she had been willing to marry her uncle. What else was she capable of? Murder? Most certainly. The blame for a long list of deaths was laid at her door. She was accused of killing political rivals, women who made her jealous with their beauty or their jewels, even people whose gardens she wanted! It was said that she sent her guards to track down her enemies and bring back their heads. One apparently arrived so decomposed that she could only confirm who it was by lifting the rotting lips and checking the teeth. So, when Claudius died in year 54, it should come as no surprise that everybody thought: Agrippina.

Death by mushroom

Poisonous and edible mushrooms are difficult to tell apart, and the Ancient Romans had no idea. (In fact, some believed that edible mushrooms could be turned toxic by exposure to an unhealthy environment or the breath of a snake.) Small wonder then that accidents were regularly reported, and that poisoning was often suspected if there was no other obvious cause of death.

Agrippina had a reputation as a poisoner. Most famously, she was rumored to have used mushrooms to kill her third husband, the emperor Claudius. Death by mushroom poisoning was not kind. Three poisonous mushrooms were used:

The symptoms of Amonita muscaria made themselves felt within two hours. Victims would experience severe abdominal pain, diarrhea, and breathing problems. They would become dizzy and confused. Delirium or convulsions would set in, followed by coma and death within hours.

The mushroom Amonita pantherina produced similar effects, but more slowly and subtly.

Amonita phalloides had even more delayed effects. Symptoms did not show for six to fifteen hours. Victims would experience abdominal pain, vomiting, and bloody diarrhea for a few days before dying.

These vague symptoms, which could be caused just as easily by food poisoning—much more common in the days before refrigeration—made accusations of mushroom poisoning almost impossible to prove or disprove. The future emperor, Domitian, wisely took matters into his own hands by absolutely refusing to eat mushrooms at all!

What she ate

What the Romans liked to eat sounds even more poisonous than mushrooms! Menus and recipes for Roman feasts have survived from Agrippina's time. It seems the Romans ate a lot of odd stuff: roasted dormice, herons' tongues, parrotfish livers, peacock and pheasant brains, camels' feet.... If you think such delicacies are scary enough, another great favorite was a sow's udders and private parts!

What's more surprising is that, despite the rumors of murder, the Romans gave their new sixteen-year-old emperor, Nero, a rapturous welcome. Just like his uncle Caligula, the handsome young man raised hopes for a second Germanicus, and gave no hint of the tyrant he would quickly become. In fact, Nero seemed to be humble and respectful—especially to his mother. He walked beside her lectica (or litter) as Agrippina was carried through the streets, and honored her with the first watchword he gave the Praetorian Guard: *optima mater*—best mother.

Nero, like Claudius, honored Agrippina on his coins, showing her as his equal and partner.

Coins © Classical Numismatic Group, Inc. http://www.cngcoins.com

What she "drove"

There were a few ways for a wealthy Roman woman to get around the city. The chiramaxium, similar to a rickshaw, was pushed by a single man, usually a slave. The sella, or sedan chair, was probably more popular with the ladies—it offered privacy and moved more comfortably and quickly, being carried by two or four slaves. The lectica, or litter, was the luxury vehicle in the streets of Rome and how Agrippina would have moved around the city. Passengers were carried in a reclining position, curtained and veiled against the envious eyes of pedestrians, surrounded by sculptures, paintings, and colorful flowers, hoisted above the crowds on the shoulders of eight slaves. Carriages were restricted to those of the State and the Vestal Virgins. Agrippina was famously granted the use of one on special occasions when Caligula gave her the same rights as the Vestal Virgins.

But this situation did not last. Nero, given absolute power and greeted daily by the adulation of the people and the Guard, didn't take long to resent the interference of his mother. And Agrippina was more than bossy and domineering. When they had disagreements, she ferociously and publicly reminded Nero that she had put him on the throne. She acted as if she, with her closer link to Emperor Augustus, was the one born with the right to rule! (The Romans couldn't think of anything more unnatural than a woman telling a man what to do.)

Things came to a head when a foreign delegation came to Rome. In sharp contrast with her role during the homage of Caratacus, no place was made for Agrippina in the ceremony. As she walked toward Nero, determined to take what she considered her rightful place in public affairs, Nero stepped off his dais to greet her. The meaning of the gesture was obvious to everyone. She was not to join him on his dais. He alone was, and would be, emperor.

THE LAST WORD

Agrippina watches the dust rise over the road. She can hear the clomp-clomp of hob-nailed boots. She narrowly escaped a near-drowning only hours earlier. She'd been returning by boat after dining with Nero when something had gone wrong. In the confusion, she'd found herself flung into the water. Any hope that this had been an accident disappeared when she found herself being battered by oars on the head and arms as she surfaced. The sailors had tried to kill her, but she had managed to swim back to shore. Now, she knows, they are coming to finish their work. And she knows it is her own son who has sent them.

She hears a step behind her, sees light running along a blade as the sword is drawn. Turning, she draws herself to her full height. Erect with the ferocious arrogance that has caused so much resentment, she raises her robes and bares her stomach. "Strike the womb that bore Nero," she commands.

How dastardly was she?

Agrippina was accused of many murders—among other dreadful things. Was she really so dastardly?

Accusation	Defense
Murdering her first two husbands	Nobody suspected Agrippina of killing her first and second husbands at the time they died. That's because there's absolutely no evidence that she did so.
Murdering Emperor Claudius	Agrippina also had little to gain from the murder of Claudius. Part of her great unpopularity was due to the fact that she was seen to rule the roost—Claudius gave her an enormous share of power, certainly more than she exercised with Nero. Also, there was a lot of scurrying around behind closed palace gates after Claudius' death. One could argue that if his death had been planned, Agrippina would have been better prepared to transfer power smoothly to Nero. Finally, the records show many public officials dying in the months before Claudius' death, presumably from an epidemic. Claudius was known to be in generally poor health, so he may have simply succumbed to one of the more unhealthy summers in Rome.
Executing her enemies without trial	Surprisingly, given her reputation, after Agrippina became empress there were fewer and fewer in camera, or closed-door, trials or executions with no trial held at all. More cases were tried openly. There was increased cooperation with, and respect for, the senate. Most of Agrippina's supposed victims were convicted in open trials. Whether these trials were entirely fair, and whether her opponents deserved execution, is another argument.